The Corridors
of
Strange Darkness

The Corridors
of
Strange Darkness

Struggling with the Experience of Glaucoma

Eugene L. Neville

RESOURCE *Publications* · Eugene, Oregon

Resource Publications
An Imprint of Wipf and Stock Publishers
199 W. 8th Ave., Suite 3
Eugene, OR 97401

www.wipfandstock.com

ISBN 13: 978-1-4982-3165-7

Manufactured in the U.S.A.   07/06/2015

The quotations from the Bible are taken from the KJV Super Giant Print Reference Bible, copyright 1996 by Broadman & Holman Publishers; NIV, copyright 1973, 1978, 1984 by International Bible Society; and NLT, copyright 1996 by Tyndale House Publishers.

But you are a chosen people, a royal priesthood, a holy nation, a people to be his very own and to proclaim the wonderful deeds of the one who called you out of darkness into his marvelous light. (1 Pet 2:9)

Contents

The Long Corridor

Rev. Eugene L. Neville

Wow! My own space.
I can run up and down the hallway all day long.
Here, nobody will tell me to be still.
I can kick my soccer ball into the next room,
No one will be there to stop me.
I can shout as loud as I can,
The only voice I will hear is my own echo.
This place is awesome!

How did I get in here?
What did I do wrong to deserve this?
What's with all these steps?
How do I get out of here?
What's behind that strange darkness?
Is that the end of the corridor?

Why am I here?
Where is the effervescent light coming from?
Is the light source real or artificial?
Are these steps descending or ascending?
What do the etchings in the arches mean?
Why is this corridor so long?
Is stepping into that strange darkness the only safe way out?

The Long Corridor

This place is so different.
The path is covered with a beautiful long red carpet.
The walls are brilliant and elegant.
The arches are fantastic!
My path is now much clearer,
I am now closer to the strange darkness.
I am not afraid. I feel so peaceful.
Wow! It's amazing!

Standing here in the midst of this strange Light
Is glorious, majestic and inexplicably beautiful!

The Lord is my Shepherd.
Even though, now I have to walk through the corridors of the Strange
    Light
I will not be afraid because now I can clearly see
God has always been with me!

Preface

NORMALLY, I AM A very private person, but having spent forty five years as a pastor I have become more transparent. My thoughts are guarded with seasoned discretion. However, at the age of seventy two, I sense the need to be even more transparent, and to humbly expose myself with the intent to encourage others to be pro-active in dealing with matters of health and spirituality. My life's journey has led me down many perplexing and sometimes painful corridors, which euphemistically I refer to as "strange darkness," even though there were reflections of light along the way. I discovered that it is only when we near the end of the final corridors of our lives that we begin to see darkness from a mature perspective.

As I contend with the challenges of growing older and especially in my struggles with glaucoma (*the silent thief of sight*), I am hopeful that my steps might serve as an inspirational source of encouragement to those who in like manner might be coping with this same ordeal or any other life-altering medical condition.

Chapter 1

The Corridor of Theological Reflection

LIFE IS A MAJESTIC and precious gift from Almighty God, extended freely to all of humanity. God created every human being equal in his sight, and decreed that everyone be granted the right to live with dignity, love, and respect. God's original destiny for humankind was declared to be "good." However, the consequence of the abject disobedience of one person (Adam) to God's life-authenticating instructions was to open a channel for evil to make its incursion into the human condition—thereby ushering in violence, sickness, and death. Consequently, throughout the corridors of time men and women, cognizant of their estrangement from the creator, have been taunted from within. Their restless souls have desperately sought to be delivered—either from self-centered religious belief systems or from their usurpation of power from those weaker than themselves. However, despite these self-generated efforts, nothing is able to remedy a deep sense of estrangement from God or bring sustainable inner healing. God is the only one who is able to restore all of creation back to its original design and purpose.

Before the foundations of the cosmos God made the restorative process for the earth possible by stepping into the human condition in the person of his one and only son, Jesus Christ. The Holy Scriptures declare, "God was in Jesus Christ reconciling the world to Himself." (2 Cor 5:19) Jesus Christ paid the ultimate price to atone for the sins of the world by vicariously suffering and dying on the cross at Calvary. His sacrifice completely satisfied the righteous justice of God. Throughout all generations if anyone places faith in the Son of God they will be forgiven for all their sins. They will be enabled by the Holy Spirit of God to live victoriously, and to experience authentic peace of mind and soul, especially in the midst of difficult situations challenging to faith.

Every person who walks on the face of earth has been endowed by God with the right to pursue each opportunity that might afford them longevity of life, peace of mind, and prosperity for themselves as well as for their families. However, for so many millions of people these rights and privileges have been denied, dashed to the ground, and shattered. Consequently, their dreams and hopes for tomorrow seem to be nothing more than illusive dreams or valleys of hopelessness. These feelings stem from several real socio-economic, emotional, and spiritual factors such as the daily intrusion of uncontrollable financial situations, the presence of painful or incurable diseases, the untimely passing of a loved one, and domestic violence or unresolved family discord. These are but a few of the etiological factors.

Moreover, living in a state of perennial pain and frustration has understandably become unbearable for some individuals. Sometimes the only option they can imagine is to give up, thereby surrendering to the strange darkness that has enshrouded their lives. The entire earth appears to be engulfed by this same darkness. Uncontrollable crises, dangerous spirits of entitlement, narcissism, self-centeredness, and self-annihilation are characteristic of this present generation. Our generation has become inundated by many global life-threatening situations. The nations of the earth are standing on the dangerous precipice of world war III. At the same time, our ears have grown weary of hearing the apocalyptic prognosticator's pronouncements about the imminent destruction of everything on the planet by anything from rogue objects from outer space to some other catastrophic event in nature. We are reminded daily of man's inhuman behavior towards others, especially with regards to the impoverished and marginalized. The constant untenable displays of violence on a global scale appear on our televisions, IPads, and other social media technologies, further exacerbating our anger.

The proliferation of injustices thrust upon people of color take the form of:

1. Inadequate provisions for people suffering from chronic, emotional, or physical illness

2. The disparity of incarceration rates among African American boys and men (and, increasingly, African American females)

3. Crimes against the homeless

4. Ineffective educational systems

5. Corrupt financial institutions

6. Insensitive religious institutions

7. Obstructionism from Congress and other political institutions

8. Dysfunctional families and the spread of terrorism around the world

9. The frequent shooting and killing of young black men in cities across America

The conjoining of these painful systematic and systemic conditions has given rise to a world-wide experience of frustration, fear, disillusionment, rage, and violence. Moreover, in my view, these societal conditions have also stolen from this generation its moral balance, dignity, and peace of mind. In their place are deposited many reasons why so many people continue to lose hope for today, and for experiencing a better life tomorrow. A strange darkness encircles the entire earth. People all around are desperately searching for prescriptions capable of bringing balance, love, and hope back to our world—a world where justice, peace, and hope will once again radiate as embraceable realities.

Into these dark, broken, and hurting places, a plethora of deeper unspoken questions still pulsate through people's minds. Aside from the perennial and unanswerable question "Why me?" many in sincerity, tearfully, and with a modicum of anger ask other questions such as:

1. Is there a medicine or medical treatment that can heal our broken hearts?

2. Are there any curative treatments that can restore our damaged emotions?

3. Are there any antidotal programs that can restore our shattered dreams for our families?

4. Is what we are experiencing today all there is to life?

5. Is life worth living?

Was Solomon, the wisest man of antiquity, correct when he referred to life as being nothing more than meaninglessness—like "chasing after the wind?"

> *I looked at everything I had worked so hard to accomplish,*
> *It was so meaningless—like chasing after the wind.*
> *There was nothing really worthwhile anywhere.* (Eccl 2:11)

Should we therefore embrace his futile perspective or the Epicurean philosophy, which in essence suggests that in light of the present uncertainties and complexities of life one should utilize one's limited moments on earth as a materialist: eating whatever one desires without regard to its unhealthy dietary ramifications; drinking as much as one is able to with no concern for the consequences; enjoying every sensual and erotic pleasure as often as one desires because we only live once and after death there is nothing else. So live licentiously, be happy until you die! If this is all there is to life, then what another ancient writer, the Apostle Paul, tells us might also be true: *"If only for this life we have hope in Christ, we are of all people most to be pitied."* (1 Cor 15:19)

However, in spite of everything, and in contrast with the natural order that appears to look hopeless and pessimistic, hope in God's promises still remains the undaunted truth. These words, penned by James Russell Lowell at another critical moment in our history still reverberate in the present moment. Eloquently he writes:

> *Though the cause of evil prosper,*
> *yet the truth alone is strong.*
> *Though her portion be the scaffold,*
> *and upon the throne be wrong,*
> *yet that scaffold sways the future,*
> *and behind the dim unknown,*
> *standeth God within the shadow*
> *keeping watch above his own.*[1]

Like countless generations that have preceded us, the human soul desperately yearns for peace and hope. However, it cannot find either until the penultimate question is answered: "Is there any reason for humankind to keep hope alive?" Finding answers to this most pressing question is not easy. In many instances, the answers might only come after passing through intense struggles or painful years of abuse, loneliness, or illness. I have learned that sometimes it is during those trying moments of anguish that God speaks and answers do come. In the midst of our unfathomable darkness, while our world is still swirling in chaos and disarray, suddenly, the glorious light of God's love, mercy, and grace bursts forth upon us and showers us with innumerable new reasons to embrace life, keeping our hope alive. Unexpectedly, our sense of dignity and meaning is restored. Once again we find ourselves clothed with inexplicable peace of mind, joy in our hearts, and miraculous healing in our minds and bodies. Somehow, God ushers us into a sacred place of authentic faith. With this renewed hope and faith, we begin to believe that no matter what unforeseeable, uncontrollable, incurable, and painful circumstance arises in our lives, life is still worth living.

Into each life trouble, sickness, or even the death of a loved one might come. No one is immune from trouble. Nevertheless, we must continue to find the inner strength to move forward with

---

1. Lowell, *Poems of James Russell Lowell*, p. 200.

hope and purpose. Always be mindful that the quality of life is not determined by how many struggles and obstacles we may have to endure. Rather, the full value of our lives will be measured by how well we embraced and lived with other people in the midst of those difficult days. The most important measuring rod to consider is our answer to the question: "Did we utilize our fleeting moments to be drawn into a closer personal relationship with Almighty God through Jesus Christ, or, did we choose to walk through the precarious challenges of life alone?"

CHAPTER 2

The Corridor of Challenges

As stated earlier, there are many life challenges and diseases that impact the lives of millions of people around the world. Life will always remain filled with a plethora of unending, enigmatic challenges. For example, while some serious diseases are curable with proper immunization and medical treatments, there remain numerous others that are incurable and have devastating outcomes. I have chosen to use this medium to share with you information about an invasive disease that is seldom discussed in the African-American or other minority communities. Nevertheless, it is one that carries, embedded within itself, life-altering physical, emotional, and spiritual realities.

Today I, as well as a large segment of people across this nation, contend daily with the silent ophthalmic disease called glaucoma. Glaucoma is a progressive eye disease that damages peripheral and central vision. If left undiagnosed and untreated, it can lead to total blindness. Glaucoma is no respecter of persons. Numerous people have become susceptible to this affliction by heredity.

There are different types of glaucoma. The most common diagnosis is called primary open-angle glaucoma. It is usually painless and has virtually no symptoms. Moreover, according to several medical research studies, glaucoma is the leading cause of blindness among millions of people, especially within the African-American and Hispanic races. Many of those with a predisposition to glaucoma do not realize they have it until it is too late. According to many leading ophthalmologists, this is why glaucoma is called, *"the silent thief of sight."* In many cases, early detection and corrective treatments might have prevented blindness in countless individuals. Therefore, annual check-ups are recommended for those diagnosed with glaucoma, and it is suggested that family members do likewise. However, there are several mitigating factors that may cause some people not to seek medical advice or give the proper attention to this or some other life-altering disease. Among these factors are:

1. Misinformation about the disease or treatment options
2. Distrust of the medical profession
3. Inadequate or no health insurance coverage
4. Major financial difficulties
5. Pride and ignorance

I know firsthand what it feels like for a person born with natural vision, now in later years, to be confronted daily with the real possibility of becoming blind. That thought became a frightening and traumatic experience. Each day I discovered unique and provocative things about my mind. Interestingly, the human mind, when confronted by the unknowable, has the capacity to conjure a plethora of strange thoughts and mental images. In some instances, depending upon one's ability to discern reality from fantasy, and one's coping mechanisms and support systems to handle disconcerting or painful information, one can easily succumb to baseless fears conjured up by one's imagination.. These negative thoughts about things that have not actually been experienced can progressively become a stronghold in our lives. Silently the mind hides and nurtures these strange notions which—sometimes years later—manifest as injurious attitudinal changes or behavioral disorders. I can attest to this from personal experience.

Many years ago, I was examined by an optometrist and was diagnosed with borderline glaucoma. I minimized its importance because there were no physical symptoms or apparent threats to my wellbeing at the time. Moreover, I had no clue as to what the term actually meant. The optometrist did not take the time to clearly explain the condition or its possible long-term outcomes relative to my overall eye health. Forty years later, because of my own lack of "self-care" and responsibility, I developed a severe ophthalmic condition attributable to glaucoma. Consequently, I am now contending with the reality of becoming totally blind. However, I am not overwhelmed by trepidation, anger, or despair.

In the next few pages, I would like to invite you to accompany me on a journey through various corridors that unfolded before me. In each corridor there were numerous challenges and awe-inspiring experiences, which in the long run helped me to better understand myself and my ophthalmic condition. In other words, each corridor enabled me to overcome numerous misconceptions that almost destroyed my chances of receiving the curative treatments I needed to normalize the aggressive advancement of glaucoma, and assisted in applying the healing balm needed for my mind's eye. I am grateful to the medical doctors and family members who rescued me before I prematurely became another statistic. With a voice of triumph, I can unapologetically testify:

I once could see,
Now I am blind.
Now, I can really see!
Thank you, Lord!

CHAPTER 3

The Corridor of Life

ON OCTOBER 4, 1942, in the city of Boston, Massachusetts, twin babies made their grand entrance into the world. They were the ninth and tenth children born into the Neville family. The meaning of their birth names would come to reflect their overall purpose and destiny. The infant girl was named Jeanette, which means, "Gift of God" and the infant boy was named Eugene, which means, "Well Born." Jeanette majestically emerged ten minutes before Eugene. She was endowed from birth with many talents and abilities. Eugene, on the other hand, entered after God made a few more character tweaks. Had Eugene been born first, perhaps his name would not have been an appropriate fit.

Several years later, three additional children were added to the Neville family, namely, Donald, John, and Marion. Although we grew up in what others refer to as the ghetto we never knew it, nor ever developed a poor mentality. Although my parents endured numerous hardships, nevertheless, they always did everything to the best of their abilities to ensure that all thirteen of their children grew up in a stable and loving home. As we grew and developed into adulthood, our parents taught each one of us by way of their example how to function with integrity, to strive towards excellence, and to press forward no matter how difficult the challenges might seem. They also instilled in us strong family values. Whatever obstacles or challenges came into our lives, we were taught to always trust in the Lord, and always seek to encourage one another. It was expected of us to work hard, and never give up on our dreams or goals.

My childhood years were the greatest. It was a time of joyful family gatherings, especially during the holidays. Playing all kinds of games (red rover, hopscotch, hide and go seek, etc.) with kids from the neighborhood, in the streets, backyards, and alley-ways, was wonderful. Fussing, teasing, and fighting with my siblings were a daily occurrence. We all had the innate ability to master the art of provoking, agitating, and manipulating. We all practiced the art of lying with a straight face. I think I mastered it the best!

The least enjoyable time was when Donald, John, Jeanette, and I all had to line up for a spanking. I believe our neighbors thought the Neville kids were having voice lessons in their house. Often a cacophony of high tones would drift out of our windows. Our neighbors soon came to find out that we were just being lined up again for a unified spanking. My mother, prior to the spanking, always made this strange announcement: "This is gonna hurt me more than it will hurt you." I never found out how much it hurt her. All I can remember is how much it hurt me! Without discussion the verdict was determined, especially if no one confessed to their misdeed. The four of us were all declared guilty. The most humiliating part of that ordeal was that each of us had to go outside to the back yard and get our own switch from the old sumac tree. At that time we did not realize that the branches of a sumac tree were poisonous, much like a vine of poison ivy. If we happened to intentionally choose a switch that would prematurely break after a few swings—"Lord have mercy." Our underpants were snatched down and over her lap we went for the prolongation of our punishment.

Somehow, mercy heard our despairing cries and stepped in just in time. During those chastening periods, we all had whelps and uncomfortable rashes all over our bodies. For days we had to cover ourselves with calamine lotion and wait until the rash disappeared. We thought our mother was the meanest woman in the world. Later we learned how much she loved all of us, and how much good came out of those episodic experiences. For the most part, the lying was curtailed; more importantly, each of us built up an immunity to poison sumac.

CHAPTER 4

The Corridor of Family Drama

ON SATURDAYS AND SUNDAYS, especially during supper time, the Neville home was often filled with the aroma of fresh baked bread and great food. Our father worked at a major restaurant as the head chef. He taught several of us the culinary arts of baking and cooking. Evenings were also eventful times in our home. Whenever we watched television, our laughter and screams probably could be heard throughout the neighborhood.

Our house was often filled with drama, especially whenever it was time for us younger kids to go to bed. None of us liked going upstairs to bed. If the truth be told, we were all afraid of the dark. It seems that all of us experienced a time when struggling with the dark was unavoidable. In my home situation, when I was about eight years old, each night, as soon as the kitchen clock rapidly approached eight o'clock, my mother shouted out, "It's almost eight o'clock! Get ready to go upstairs, it's time for bed! School's in the morning!" Like most kids, we pretended not to hear her voice and kept watching television because our favorite program, *The Adventures of Mr. Magoo*, was not completely over. However, as soon as it ended, with a discordant note in her voice, she came back into the small living room and shouted, "Didn't I say go upstairs and go to bed? Go, now!" Obediently, we all stopped what we were doing, turned off the television, and stomped upstairs to our rooms. We each had our separate reasons for not wanting to go to bed: "I'm not tired!," "It's still early!," and "I can't go to sleep!" We all cried. I think I protested the most but to no avail.

In the bedroom I remember keeping the small table lamp on for as long as possible. Every night we each had the uneasy feeling that something scary or strange was hiding in the dark. Whether it was under our beds, in the closet, or in the shadows on the walls, we were certain that something was just waiting for us to fall asleep to do us harm in the night. The lamp shed just enough light to illuminate the room, even if it was only for a moment. Quickly, the three of us boys jumped into the bed and with our eyes wide open whispered the prayer our mother taught us long ago:

> *Now I lay me down to sleep, I pray the Lord my soul to keep.*
> *If I should die before I wake, I pray the Lord my soul to take.*

As a child I was not sure what that little prayer meant, but it worked because we all made it through each night. It was in my childhood bedroom where I think I began to learn how to wrestle with the strange products of my imagination that were hiding in the darkness.

I remember vividly, especially during the winter months, how a cold breeze whistled into our room through spaces between the windows, accompanied by flickering moon beams that pierced through the partially closed window curtains. The appearance of weird shadows suddenly cascaded on the bedroom walls. We each saw them as different creatures, and began to describe them as they appeared. The weird images were intensified by the intermittent popping sounds coming from the hot water radiator pipes. Suddenly all of these strange things came together and scared us, causing us to throw the covers over our heads. We certainly believed that the creatures cascading upon the walls were trying their best to get out. Slowly I stretched out my arm from beneath the covers and quickly turned the small table lamp back on. Immediately the small light chased the creatures away. Against my will, I eventually surrendered myself to the dimness and fell asleep. My bedroom might have just been the starting place or first corridor of my wrestling match with the strange darkness.

CHAPTER 5

The Corridor
of Strange Darkness

SIBLING RIVALRY HAS ITS consequences. My brother Joseph—my elder by three years— and I were always in mortal combat. We both knew how to get on each other's last nerve. When I was about ten years old, for several nights just as I was about to fall into a deep sleep, Joseph would sneak into the bedroom and from the bottom of my bed gradually pull the covers off of me. The sensation petrified me so much that I dared not move or fall asleep. I thought the monsters in the walls finally got out and were coming to snatch me away. Slowly I turned over and attempted to switch the lamp back on, but it would not turn on, because my brother had loosened the light bulb.

At other times Joseph would crawl from underneath my bed and rub the fur from a stuffed animal on my hands and growl. This time, I was sure that a wild animal was in the room. Again I was petrified, and remained frozen throughout much of the night. The next morning, I learned that Joseph was the culprit. Thereafter, I kept the small table lamp on all night, just in case. I often wondered, as with other complicated relationships in our lives, if my brother unknowingly contributed to my lifetime struggle with the strange darkness that awaited me.

CHAPTER 6

The Corridor of Transition

IT IS INTERESTING TO note how thoughts, behavior patterns, and belief systems follow us from childhood into adolescence. When I became a teenager, many of my childhood assumptions, attitudes, apprehensions, and aspirations took a radical turn. The frightful and distorted images that were once cascading on my bedroom walls became realities of a different sort. It was as though phantoms imprisoned inside the bedroom wall had escaped and continued to pursue me as transformative and challenging realities. These new realities, birthed from that darkness, made indelible imprints on my mind and perceptions about life. The strange darkness engulfed me like a mighty rushing storm, and embroiled within me an anger that sometimes ran very deep. It began to affect my behavior, how I treated others, and how adversely I thought about myself.

Throughout my adolescent years, my soul was often disquieted by perennial challenges to choose either the path of darkness or the way of light. Should I believe in ethereal truths or accept unverifiable myths? Should I embrace invisible hope or yield to the dark spirit of helplessness? Would I walk circumspectly or live iniquitously? Ultimately, I felt compelled to choose whether to live or to die. With all of these strange thoughts and assumptions, I felt as though I had unwillingly been driven into the corridor of bitterness and anger.

CHAPTER 7

The Corridor of Anger

SOMETHING INTERNAL AND VITALLY important to the positive development of my character was being radically altered, and was replaced with indiscriminate anger and self-hatred. Several times the depth of this anger was manifested whenever I was in conflict with my brothers or friends.

On one specific occasion, when I was about thirteen, I became angry with one of my brothers and started a fist fight. I am not sure what precipitated the argument, but I became so enraged that I went into the kitchen with the premeditated intent to do him bodily harm. I placed a large pot of water on the stove, waiting patiently for it to come to the boiling point. Then I approached him and threw it at him. Fortunately for both of us, most of the hot water missed him. He was not seriously burned. I felt that I taught him a lesson and to leave me alone. I was blind to the consequences of my vengeful actions. I had not considered that he could have been scarred for life, and that I would have been sent to jail. However, judgment and punishment came later that evening from the hands of my father.

Pain in the soul manifests itself in many ways. To the untrained eye or inattentive observer, pain veils itself with smiles and sometimes with an invisible mask, hiding a repressed raging spirit. Beneath the surface and beyond natural eyesight there is something like a turbulent volcano, ready to explode at the slightest provocation and from which no one is safe.

Paul Lawrence Dunbar accurately and articulately conveys these hidden, conflictive feelings that were not only within me, but also submerged in the life experiences of countless African-American men and women. He wrote:

> We wear the mask that grins and lies,
> It hides our cheeks and shades our eyes,
> This debt we pay to human guile;
> With torn and bleeding hearts we smile,
> And mouth with myriad subtleties,
> We smile, but, O great Christ, our cries to thee
> From tortured souls arise
> We sing, but oh the clay is vile beneath our feet,
> And long the mile; but let the world dream otherwise
> We wear the mask![1]

Today, it saddens me to recall the following incident. When I was sixteen years old, at home, my brother Joseph and I were engaged in a conflict beyond our self-control points. He punched me in the face and caused my eye to swell. In my moment of utter rage, I ran into the kitchen, picked up a sharp butcher knife and threw it at him. The knife missed him only by a few inches and stuck into the wall. I missed him intentionally that time. From that day forward, neither he nor I ever again engaged in that level of uncontrollable contention. That dangerous encounter vividly demonstrated to us that deep-seated anger had the capacity to thrust us into doing life-threatening things. The possibility of seriously injuring or killing my brother propelled me into a path of unimaginable guilt, a place where I knew I did not belong nor wanted to be. Little did I know that my descent into this corridor of strange darkness was becoming a seemingly impenetrable stronghold in my life.

The anger within me did not decrease because I did not know how to forgive those who hurt me. The feeling of anger seemed to

---

1. Braxton, *The Collected Poetry of Paul Lawrence Dunbar*, p. 71.

intensify as I interacted with my peers in high school and around the neighborhood. I was beginning to act and feel like Dr. Jekyll and Mr. Hyde. In my moments of solitude I often wondered: where did all of this anger, rage, and self-hatred come from? For the most part, I thought of myself as being a very sensitive and introverted person. However, on the other hand, if I felt or knew that I was mistreated, lied upon, or if I thought my good intentions were intentionally being misconstrued, an immediate eruption was imminent. Some of my closest associates renamed me "Neville the devil." I am sure some of my brothers and sisters would have agreed with this revised designation.

The phantoms of the dark infiltrated the strata of my mind. This became pronounced when I was a high school student. It was not because I had been bullied by other students. Rather, it was when, for the first time in my life, I actually came face to face with segregation and institutionalized racism. Like so many other black high school students in the late 50s, I was instructed each year by the guidance counselor not to register for advanced classes or college level courses. Why? Because she determined that I would not be able to compete with the white students, nor retain the skill sets necessary to succeed. This was not based on my academic performance through the years, but rather entirely upon my racial distinctiveness. Therefore, I was restricted to pursue a trade and systematically directed away from taking basic courses such as algebra, foreign languages, or courses that required critical thinking. These courses were declared to be outside of my range of possibility. By way of comparison, several of the white kids with whom I grew up, whose mental acuity was no greater than mine, were admitted into those same areas of study from which I was excluded.

Moreover, I watched the white people in my community get preferential treatment relative to employment opportunities and to matters of law and punishment. Needless to say, when similar infractions to the law were committed by both ethnic groups, those of us who were black were either beaten, shot to death, incarcerated, or charged with a felony. The white counterparts were rarely arrested or charged with anything. Even with my limited knowledge of the laws relative to equity and justice, I intuitively understood that those practices were unfair and unjust. Prejudice and blatant injustice has the capacity to thrust anyone into injurious and socially unacceptable behavior.

Interestingly, in all of my dysfunctional adolescent years, I never aligned myself with gang activity or radical organizations. Though the invitation was always open, I did not want to bear the consequences within my family of intentionally violating household regulations, nor did I want to be shot to death at the hand of a rogue police officer or a confused gang member. Nor was the temptation to experiment with drugs, smoke marijuana, or drink alcohol a viable option. I was reminded every day of the devastating effects of addiction, lived out by those staggering drunk on the street corners or lying sick in the alleys. Even though I had several girlfriends, sexual activity was discouraged by the real fear of contracting sexually transmitted disease. The experiences of several of my close friends were enough of a deterrent for me. All of these temptations and subsequent consequences were ever present realities in my sphere of life.

CHAPTER 8

The Corridor of Correction

LIKE MANY OF MY peers, I too could have been incarcerated, or killed and buried in a lowly grave. What saved me? What rescued me from utter self-destruction? I believed and still believe it was the divine intervention of God, and recalling to memory the core values instilled in me during childhood—in particular, the prayers and corrective measures systematically administered to me by the hands of my mother and older sister Gertrude. I learned the hard way, that they were the Lord's administrators, specifically appointed to reset the default buttons of my life every time I was out of order or character.

My mother and oldest sister both had strong hands! When I was a child, I had many vivid episodes with Gertrude. Today, when I recall those special memories, I cannot keep myself from laughing. However, at the time they were quite painful. I think my sister took very seriously that old adage, *"Do not withhold discipline from a child; if you punish them with the rod, they will not die."* (Prov 23:13) I recall the in-house track meets in which Gertrude and I were engaged. We would run throughout the house, in and out of every room, up and down the hallway stairs. We even crawled under the beds. She was always right there beside me, grabbing, and shouting, "Gene, don't you run away from me! Wait until I get my hands on you!"

She always managed to catch me. I used to think she had placed a belt in every room just for me because no matter where I ran, whenever she needed it, the belt always showed up. A most memorable event was the day Gertrude chased me all the way down into the dark basement of our house. She must have had the gift of night vision. No matter where I ran or tried to hide she always found me. Screaming, I hid behind the furnace and she found me! Screaming, I ran between and around the brick posts and she saw me! Screaming, I ran into the coal shed and she located me! Finally, I tried running up the stairs, hollering at the top of my lungs: it did not matter. She caught me! The event in the dark basement began. The belt was moving a hundred miles per minute for what seemed to be ten minutes. In the midst of my screaming in the darkness of those moments, I do not know how she did it. Somehow the movement of the belt was in perfect sync with her mantra, "Didn't I tell you never to run away from me?" That day, in the darkness of the basement, I finally learned several very important life lessons:

1. When in trouble do not run: stand still and bear the consequences.
2. Weeping may last for thirty minutes, but that too will pass.
3. Last but not least, never upset your older sister.

In later years I surmised that either I was an incorrigible kid or my sister just needed to get her weekly exercise. I further discovered how my older brothers became great track stars and athletic contenders. It was attributable to Gertrude's proverbial belt! She had even given it a permanent name: "Egor."

Those were the days when many black families took common, acceptable measures to correct their loved ones. Even though corporal punishment today is looked at with disdain, nonetheless, I appreciate my parents and older siblings because they helped to reshaped so many of my propensities to do wrong.

CHAPTER 9

The Corridor of Fear

I COULD NOT WAIT until I reached my twenties. I thought life would be different and I waited for the time to come in which I would be free to do whatever I determined without permission or impunity. However, those years I found to be most challenging and disconcerting. I made several unwise decisions which most young men in their twenties are prone to do.

Some of my choices led to paths of loneliness, fear of failure, and confusion. It seemed as though life had become unfulfilling and meaningless. Gradually, my soul was being drawn into real cycles of despair. Unknowingly, I was beginning to project my feelings of failure and inadequacy upon others. Even though I attended weekly church services, I nevertheless still wondered where God was and why He did not answer my silent prayers. At that time in my life, I could easily identify with the pathos pressed out in the despairing cry of the psalmist:

> *Lord, you are the God who saves me;*
> *day and night I cry out to you.*
> *May my prayer come to you;*
> *turn your ear to my cry.*
> *I am overwhelmed with troubles*
> *and my life draws near to death.*

I am counted among those who go down to the pit;
I am like one without strength.
I am set apart with the dead,
like the slain who lie in the grave,
whom you remember no more,
who are cut off from your care.
You have put me in the lowest pit,
in the darkest depths.
Your wrath lies heavily on me;
you have overwhelmed me with all your waves.
You have taken from me my closest friends
and have made me repulsive to them.
I am confined and cannot escape;
my eyes are dim with grief. I call to you, Lord, every day;
I spread out my hands to you.
Do you show your wonders to the dead?
Do their spirits rise up and praise you?
Is your love declared in the grave,
your faithfulness in Destruction?
Are your wonders known in the place of darkness,
or your righteous deeds in the land of oblivion? But I cry to
you for help, Lord;
in the morning my prayer comes before you.
Why, Lord, do you reject me
and hide your face from me?
From my youth I have suffered and been close to death;
I have borne your terrors and am in despair.
Your wrath has swept over me;
your terrors have destroyed me.
All day long they surround me like a flood;
they have completely engulfed me.
You have taken from me friend and neighbor,
darkness is my closest friend. (Ps 88)

CHAPTER 10

The Corridor of Unrest

THROUGHOUT THE 60S AND 70S social unrest not only erupted in the city of Boston, Massachusetts, but in urban cities throughout the United States of America. National protests over the war in Vietnam, raging riots in the streets of urban communities, and the assignation of great leaders led to major civil unrest throughout the land. Even more close to home an internal, escalating war was also raging in my mind, tossing me to and fro. One moment I was feeling rage and self-hatred, and the next, I was calling out to anyone who would help me find meaning and purpose in living. It appeared that no one heard me, and the strange darkness was winning the battle of my mind. I felt myself sinking deeper into the corridor of restlessness.

The painful realities associated with finding employment as an African-American man was a vexing eye opener. I came to see first-hand how much the city of my birth had become entrenched by the ravaging effects of systemic and institutionalized racism. Each time I sought to secure a job in the city of Boston, the strange darkness of racism would emerge. What had been the painful experience of countless others was now happening to me. Whenever I responded to a job opening by telephone, it was available. However, when I appeared for the interview, I would be told by the interviewer that the job has just been filled. When I eventually acquired full-time employment, the work expectations of me were twice as demanding than for others who happened to be of a different hue. The opportunities for advancement in the company were minimal. For the most part we were denied access to advancement, not because our job performance, but primarily because of our racial distinctions.

My rage was further intensified, attributable to the practice of racial profiling by rogue police officers and uncaring and corrupt lawyers. Those official servants, who were designated and assigned to be protectors of law, order, and justice, became the purveyors of inequity and injustice. The words penned long ago by Josiah Gilbert Holland was an applicable cry of my community: *"Freedom weeps, wrong rules the land and waiting justice sleeps."*[1] Needless to say, the seeds of distrust and discord were deeply rooted and watered by the complexities of those days. I completely understand the reasons why many of my generation arose to stand up against all manner of social injustices. Some resolved to use violent means to justify their frustrations, while countless others chose the path of nonviolent resistance. Those were chaotic, dangerous, and painful times. Injustice compelled everyone to decide which path they would follow. Dr. Martin Luther King, Jr. was correct when, from a Birmingham jail on April 16, 1963 he wrote, *"Injustice anywhere is a threat to justice everywhere."*[2] Encumbered by these situations and circumstances, I was being thrust into another corridor that unknowingly provided me with wise counsel.

1. Holland, *Garnered Sheaves: the Complete Poetical Works of J. G. Holland*, p. 377.

2. Washington, *A Testament of Hope: the Essential Writings of Speeches of Martin Luther King, Jr.*, p. 290.

CHAPTER 11

The Corridor of Wise Counsel

THERE IS A DANGEROUS dimension to the darkness, which if left unchallenged, has the capacity to thrust anyone into a permanent state of helplessness, discord, hopelessness, and death. In my struggle to find meaning and purpose during those turbulent years, the Lord stepped into my chaos just in time. He progressively guided me back to the path of emotional wholeness and authentic faith. The etymological significance of my birth name—"Well Born"—became like a loud reverberating cymbal, beckoning me to reconsider my ways.

I began to recall the prayers and tough love administered to me by my mother and my sister Gertrude. The valuable survival lessons and words of wisdom taught to me long ago by my father, and other older wise men, surged like a river saturating every fiber of my mind with life-sustaining truths. I clearly recalled the essence of their wise counsel, instructing me "not to forget to remember" that when uncontrollable and untimely circumstances come and thrust me to the lowest precipices of darkness, not to fear. Even if I feel the tension of something tugging, as if it were trying to conquer my soul, it cannot! If I believe that God is always present with me in the midst of the darkness, I will find the faith and confidence to remain standing. Furthermore, they said that the darkness is also the place where I would find peace of mind. It is *"there"* where I would develop authentic faith in Almighty God. It is *"there"* where I would be transformed and transferred into the marvelous light of Jesus Christ. It is *"there"* where I would be empowered by the Holy Spirit to live victoriously over the vicissitudes of life. I wished I had followed their words of wise counsel. I had failed, but one thing I would always remember is the final word of my father before he died. He told me, "Don't fear the darkness, but always trust in God in whom even the deepest darkness is light." That is wise counsel I will always try to remember.

When I was in my early-twenties I came to understand the true meaning of their counsel. Two life-threatening ordeals intruded into my life. Each of them radically changed me and once again reset and reconfigured my priorities and out-of-skew perceptions.

One Friday evening in September, 1963, my sister Jeanette and I were walking to a house party. During those times it was not unusual for anyone to "crash a party" (attend without an invitation). While walking down a dimly lit street in the hood of Roxbury, out of the shadows of the darkness six gang members came from behind, and encircled us. One of the gang members I knew from beforehand to be crazy and dangerous. He pulled out a stiletto (a sharp knife) and put it to my throat, demanding that I give him my money. Out of pure fear I lied and said, "I don't have any." The truth of the matter was that earlier during the day I had cashed my paycheck, and kept the money in my back pocket. I did not realize that I had also kept a lot of loose change in my front pockets. Here I was, standing in the dark, with a knife pressed up against my throat, and my knees were trembling. During this time I had my hands in my front pockets, stupidly jingling the loose change. The gang member got up even closer in my face and shouted, "Man, I'm gonna kill you! Give me your . . . money!" Out of sheer panic, I frantically prayed in my heart, "Lord, help me." Just then a voice came piercing out of the darkness, "Don't hurt him. That's Neville, I know him from school, and he's ok." The one who miraculously intervened that night was Billy, who was the gang's president. I tightly embraced him, and clutched his hand with the traditional Black Hand shake. With trembling in my voice I softly said, "Thanks man!" My sister and I nervously continued down the street to the house party. Needless to say, throughout the remaining weekend my mind was immersed with serious thoughts about the ramifications of that dangerous Friday night. I could have been killed, and there was no telling what frightening things they could have done to my sister.

The second intervention took place one Saturday in June, 1964. It occurred in a pool hall located in my home turf on Blue Hill Avenue. As I recall, it was a Saturday evening at about eight thirty in the evening. I was shooting pool with a few of my friends and minding my own business. I was completely unaware that a young man came from behind me, placed a gun to my back, and told me to leave with him. I did not know him nor had I ever seen him before that evening. I assumed that his intent was to rob me. Literally, I didn't have a dime in my pocket. I was stumbling as I reluctantly walked leaving the pool hall with him. With the gun still being pressed hard against my back, I suddenly heard a very loud and a familiar voice pulsating through the room: "Don't you dare bother him, you . . . punk. Get the hell out of here before I blow off your . . . Head." It seemed as though everyone in the room took notice and started running in my direction. I felt the lowering of the gun. The young man ran out of the door cursing as several brothers chased after him. It was my longtime friend, Bobby, who shout out and saved me. Bobby was a person whom everyone respected, and knew not to contend with because of his violent temper and large family ties with the community. He saw the fear of death openly displayed on my face and without hesitation took the time to console me. Afterwards, he drove me to the safety of my home.

In each of those dangerous and life-threatening situations, after prayerful introspection, I came to realize that my life was spared by the miraculous intervention of God who had placed men who were real friends at the right place and time. God heard my faint cries and simple prayers, and literally rescued me from all manner of impending death.

Soon thereafter, the gospel was clearly explained to me by my other older sister, Evelyn. I accepted the truth of the gospel and received Jesus Christ as my Lord and Savior. I understood that he paid the full price on the cross at Calvary to deliver me from all my sins. Progressively, he led me out of that strange corridor of darkness, and spiritually translated me into his marvelous light, just like my father and other wise men said. In time, I noticed that the Lord healed my mind from many of the injurious thoughts that were continuously streaming in and out of it. The Lord replaced the darkness of fears with faith. I noticed that the deep-seated anger and self-hatred dissipated in the effulgent presence of love and hope. I discovered for myself that it was impossible for a person to commit himself to Christ and not experience character and perceptual changes in his life. New changes came into my life, and began to prepare me for sequential experiences that would not only teach me how to withstand the vicissitudes of life, but also overcome the fear factors associated with the "silent thief of vision" known as *glaucoma*.

CHAPTER 12

The Corridor of New Life

THE LIGHT SHINES BRIGHTEST in the darkest of nights. However, if the darkness of evil is not challenged, it has the capacity to thrust anyone into the depths of depression and unimaginable despair and hopelessness. No person can live a meaningful life without love and hope.

Even as Christians, the strange darkness of loneliness leaves us, but only for a season until another vulnerable moment opens. In my lonely moments, when I had reached my mid-twenties, the strange darkness reappeared to attack my mind. My life became consumed with an insatiable desire to understand my purpose and to fulfill my destiny in life. I felt so alone and empty and I needed a real friend. The Lord intervened and provided me with two people who were filled with compassion and wisdom to help and to guide me. At that pivotal moment in my life two of my old Sunday school teachers, Mr. Herbert Grandy and Mrs. Bernetha Floyd, were ushered back into my life. I recall, just as though it was yesterday, walking late at night down the dark streets of Roxbury, sometimes over eight miles, seeking wisdom and spiritual insights from Mr. Grandy. He was a strong and highly opinionated man, astute in the Bible, and conversant with every facet of urban life. Sometimes, we discussed issues throughout the night until the rising of the sun.

From our dialogue sessions, I discovered valuable life lessons that helped to reshape and elevate my self-esteem.

At other times, whenever I felt discouraged, or my mind was encumbered by discordant notes, jangled thoughts, or perplexing questions; the Lord led me once again to an awesome woman of God—Mrs. Beneatha Floyd—whom I called my "spiritual mother." On many occasions, I walked approximately five miles to her home. She always greeted me as her son and seemed to know what was needed to bring quiet to my soul. Each time she would read to me words of encouragement from the Bible, and accentuate it with a gospel song or an old "negro spiritual." To this day those old songs sometimes gently arise into my spirit. I will always be grateful to my two "ministering angels" who helped me to walk with circumspection and confidence through that perplexing strange corridor. I felt ready to exercise my new-found faith.

CHAPTER 13

The Corridor of Faith

THE APOSTLE PAUL, IN his letters to the Romans and to the Corinthians, states two of the essential action steps we must undertake if we are to be victorious in our walk of faith. He writes:

> Do not conform to the pattern of this world, but be transformed by the renewing of your mind. Then you will be able to test and approve what God's will is—his good, pleasing and perfect will. Rom 12:2

> For though we walk in the flesh, we do not war after the flesh, for the weapons of our warfare are not carnal, but mighty through God to the pulling down of strong holds, casting down imaginations, and every high thing that exalteth itself against the knowledge of God, and bringing into captivity every thought to the obedience of Christ. (2 Cor 10:3)

During those transitional years, my faith was being refined. I was learning new things about the spiritual dynamics of faith, and different ways to overcome the strange darkness of fear in many of its dimensions. My entire being began to experience a new form of restlessness. My desire to become proactively engaged within my community's struggles for equity and justice was intensified.

The examples set by spiritual and socially conscious black men and women provided me with a new perspective regarding my rich cultural heritage.

I was greatly inspired by the remarkable life examples and provocative writings of the late Rev. Dr. Martin Luther King, Jr. In his book *Strength to Love*, the truisms he penned helped me tremendously in my quest to find meaning and purpose. Those words to this day remain indelibly imprinted on my mind:

> *I would urge you to give priority to the search for God. Allow his Spirit to permeate your being. To meet the difficulties and challenges of life you will need him. Before the ship of your life reaches its last harbor, there will be long, drawn-out storms, howling and jostling winds, and tempestuous seas that make the heart stand still. If you do not have a deep and patient faith in God, you will be powerless to face the delays, disappointments, and vicissitudes that inevitably come. Without God, all of our efforts turn to ashes and our sunrises into darkest nights. Without him, life is a meaningless drama in which the decisive scenes are missing. But with him, we are able to rise from tension-packed valleys to the sublime heights of inner peace, and find radiant stars of hope against the nocturnal bosom of life's most depressing nights. St. Augustine was right: "Thou hast created us for thyself, and our heart cannot be quieted till it find repose in thee.*[1]

I chose no longer to conform to the behavior patterns of the world. Instead I decided to embrace those positive principles, examples, and teachings of Jesus Christ and of those strong men and women of God who preceded me.

1. King, *Strength to Love*, p.

CHAPTER 14

The Corridor of Academia

CAN ANY GOOD THING come out of Roxbury? Yes, in the fall of 1965, in spite of poor academic high school grades and the insensitive prognostications of the guidance counselors, I was provided with an opportunity to pursue a college degree at Barrington College in Rhode Island. This was an act of God's grace. The strange corridor of academia was an entirely new journey. Every fiber of my being was stretched and re-aligned.

My first year of college was "mind blowing." I was expected to learn a biblical language (Greek), write numerous term papers, and complete written exams. I was expected to be in dialogue with students in areas of philosophy, psychology, and theology. I had often felt insecure because I believed them to be more prepared in critical thinking than I was. It was very challenging having to eat meals in a cafeteria with students who intentionally segregated themselves from me and others because of our ethnicity. Weekly chapel services were mandatory. The music and messages were extremely boring and insensitive to my cultural heritage and church experiences. It was during those college years that I learned how to overcome the strange phenomenon known as "*Christian Racism.*"

The confluence of all of those experiences eventually contributed to the re-alignment of my self-esteem. It enabled and prepared me to face the challenges and obstacles of another year without self-deprecation or fear. Several powerful declarations became my daily mantra, including the edifying words of Saint Paul, *"I can do all things through Christ who strengthens me."* (Phil 4:13) and the words penned long ago by poet laureate, Henry Wadsworth Longfellow:

> *The Heights by great men reached and kept were not obtained by sudden flight but, while their companions slept, they were toiling upward in the night.*[1]

I made it to my junior year. That same year, surprisingly, I was voted to be the junior class president. It was diligent study throughout each night, and fervent prayer, that kept me focused on becoming the person whom God designed. The overall college experience was therapeutic and academically fulfilling. I achieved academic success, and was able to develop essential life skills that would draw me closer to my destiny. The various leadership positions provided the opportunity to network with many of the "movers and shakers" of campus life—thereby equipping me to later serve in a wide array of leadership capacities.

In 1969 I graduated with honors and a Bachelor of Arts degree. Moreover, I was amazed to learn that upon graduation, I was selected to be listed in *Who's Who in American Colleges and Universities*. The strange darkness left for a season! Upon graduation, I was afforded the opportunity to matriculate at Gordon-Conwell Theological Seminary. I was given a full three-year tuition scholarship through the collaborative efforts of Rev. Dr. Michael E. Haynes, pastor of the historic Twelfth Baptist Church located in Roxbury, Massachusetts, and Rev. Dr. Harold J. Ockenga, president of the seminary.

The experiences of those days were invaluable. They catapulted me into a depth of spiritual exhilaration and fulfillment

---

1. McClatchy, *Henry Wadsworth Longfellow: Poems and Other Writings*, p. 313.

beyond my expectation. I was immersed in many complex and sometimes incontrovertible biblical and theological realities. The length, depth, and height of my core beliefs were solidified. I found my passion in the study of Christian theology and biblical studies. My life was filled with great expectations. The desire to teach and to help others rise above their brokenness and undesired circumstances created in me an insatiable desire to do more. In retrospect, I know that it was God's grace and caring professors who guided me through the strangeness of those days.

CHAPTER 15

The Corridor of Blessing

ON AUGUST 28, 1970 I was blessed to marry my college sweetheart, Ruth Ellis. This holy union was the starting point of a long journey down the corridor of fresh blessings being poured into my life. Several years passed and we were privileged to bring two beautiful daughters into the world—Evette and Evonne. Watching them develop through the years into dynamic women of faith, they became excellent daughters who brought great joy into my life. One of the greatest blessings to receive in old age is to behold the birth, and rapid growth and development of your grandchildren. The Old Testament book of Proverbs says that *"grandchildren are the crowning glory of the aged, parents are the pride of their children."* Ruth and I were crowned with five grandchildren—Moné, Milan, Jalyn, Zachariah, and Jasmine. As a loving family, like many, we have experienced a multiplicity of blessings, disappointments, achievements, setbacks, health issues, financial issues, and relationship challenges. However, the Lord has seen us through them all. God kept us strong, loving, and committed to His promises. My immediate family has been the primary source of encouragement. They enabled me to continue my journey through the corridors of strange darkness.

In 1972, I was blessed to graduate with an earned Master of Divinity degree with honors. Soon thereafter, the insatiable desire to teach and to help others transitioned into an unquenchable strange fire in my soul. This strange fire was not frightening or painful, but it continuously saturated every fiber of my being, infusing it with a love for people. I had never experienced anything like this before. Daily, I sensed the hand of God upon my life. One day I was convinced that God had called me to preach and teach the gospel of Jesus Christ. My assignment was to reach out with arms of compassion and words of hope to the lost, the broken, the sick and the dying—people who were just like me. I felt compelled by the love of God to go wherever the need was the greatest and where the human hurt was the deepest. This now led me to a new corridor—the Corridor of Ministry.

Chapter 16

The Corridor of Ministry

CAN ANY GOOD THING come out of Roxbury? Yes: in the month of December, 1973, I was ordained a Christian minister. I was granted my first assignment as the minister of youth at the historic Twelfth Baptist Church in Roxbury, Massachusetts. Under the pastoral leadership of Dr. Michael E. Haynes, I was afforded a plethora of invaluable opportunities in which I could exercise my teaching gifts, expand my leadership abilities, and minister to people of all ethnic backgrounds, and socio-political and religious persuasions. To serve in a ministerial capacity for ten years in my birth community was an unmeritorious privilege and blessing. While serving in my home community, each challenging experience was preparing me for the new sequential corridors that were to come in the city of Brockton, Massachusetts and surrounding communities.

CHAPTER 17

The Corridor of Change

THE BEST OF TIMES and the worst of times occurred from 1975 through October 1981. It was a time of God's favor, as well as a time of heightened demonic activity. It was a time of excitement and growth, and a time of decaying trust. It was a time of hopeful expectations, and of gross darkness. Unexpectedly, the darkness unveiled its strange connectivity to many "Christian" people whom I trusted. However, no matter how pervasive and dark those moments were, they did not have the capacity to eradicate the awesome effulgence of Christ's love for me.

Pastors are not immune to trouble. Often they are the central targets of temptation and evil. The pastoral experiences of many, when placed in juxtaposition with mine, may be similar. However, some experiences are spiritually unique and particular to a local congregation. The strange darkness of those years had transfigured into real, localized manifestations. I thought those days were the most faith—stretching and emotionally stressful experiences in my life. It appeared to me as though a confluence of all the strange images from my past had traversed through a space–time portal. It appeared as if these images had formed an unholy alliance in the minds of a few spiritually detached members of our congregation. It only took a few people to turn my world upside down. However, although I had my ups and downs, I went through another corridor of good experiences before entering into a corridor of bad times.

CHAPTER 18

The Corridor of Good Times

THE FIRST FIVE YEARS of my ministry in the city of Brockton were blessed by phenomenal growth, and spiritual development. It was the best of times. The church grew from seventy members to over three hundred active congregants. The sanctuary only had a maximum seating capacity for one hundred people. As a temporary measure to accommodate the overflow of people, and to avoid city ordinance violations, we eventually renovated the small area in the church basement. Several months later, we purchased and renovated a vacant tire store located adjacent to the church. Architectural plans were developed and approved by the congregation and the City Planning Board. During the next few years we were engaged in raising funds to construct a new building, which would be adequate to accommodate our expanding ministries.

In the month of February, 1981, in anticipation of Holy Week, an interim team of church leaders was formed and assigned to locate a facility within the community—a facility that had the capacity to sufficiently accommodate the Holy Week services. As a congregation, we knew that if we could not find a site it would necessitate the conducting of three overcrowded services, instead of the traditional two services. In April, to our amazement, a beautiful church complex situated just around the corner was made available to us for a minimal monetary gift of two hundred and twenty five dollars per month. This was used to defray the custodial and utility expenses. What a blessing! The church complex had the capacity to seat approximately five hundred people in the sanctuary. Moreover, a very large lower auditorium, an industrial kitchen, and numerous classrooms and office spaces were in the building. Unknown to us, the building, which was owned by another congregation, stood vacant for five years and was meticulously maintained. Amazingly, it had everything we needed to conduct our services in one place and at the same time of day. The church leaders of that facility were delighted to have a Christian church to occupy their building. They believed in our ministry and therefore extended to us the opportunity to use the church for as long as we chose, along with the same remuneration request. Moreover, if the building was suitable to our needs, we were granted the option to purchase it for an extremely low price.

Over two hundred members of the congregation joined with me on a walk through the facility. After the walk–through they unanimously voted to occupy the facility. The Darwin and Kelley families united with my family to cover the monthly expenses for a year with no added financial strain upon the church's fund-raising efforts. Our congregation, for the first time in many years, was able to worship together as one family in Christ during Holy Week. However, our time of rejoicing was temporarily thwarted by unnecessary controversy and self-inflicted pain by a few members. The best of times was quickly turning into the worst of times. The strange darkness emerged again with vengeful, ferocious, and fallacious accusations in the midst of the most sacred of times, "Holy Week."

CHAPTER 19

The Corridor of Bad Times

ON GOOD FRIDAY, MANY church leaders and I unexpectedly received a summons to appear in court. This court hearing was to address charges orchestrated by an associate staff leader and a few disassociated senior members of the church. The charges accused leadership of misdirecting building funds to use for renting another church facility. In their minds this was a violation of church policy. Fortunately, the charge was dismissed by the judge because the accusers were not present at the church meeting to hear that certain members had consented to cover all rental expenses. They were not aware that the usage of building funds was never a part of this temporary effort. We concluded that this concern was based entirely upon the dissemination of incomplete and wrong information. The concerns could have been easily resolved outside of the court. The experience was an embarrassment to the church community and a personal disappointment.

We thought that the matter was resolved. However, the strange darkness shifted to a deeper and a more nefarious level. In the month of May, the church members voted to continue the temporary occupancy of the facility. The church also decided to accelerate the process of thoroughly analyzing all of the factors that would determine the feasibility of constructing a new edifice, instead of purchasing the rental complex. In the midst of our feasibility studies, for a period of five months, a series of malicious letters were circulated throughout the city. False charges were filed by the same disgruntled people. Each time, a court appearance was required. The judges always dismissed the charges because it was determined that the accusations were baseless and mean-spirited. The strange darkness had reappeared within me. The feelings of anger and rage, which I thought were under control, were indefatigably trying to resurface. If I did not control those feelings, the worst of times for those individuals was ready to happen. The church had never known or seen that side of me. There was no telling how my long incarcerated anger and rage would be manifested. I knew that on every side I was being pressed to the breaking point, and "Neville the devil" was impatiently crouched on the perimeter waiting to be released.

CHAPTER 20

The Corridor of Deliverance

THE WORST OF TIMES culminated during a called church meeting conducted on the first Saturday in October, 1981. Paradoxically, the first Sunday in October, 1981, became the best of times. God moved in mysterious and majestic ways to deliver his children from all manner of evil and sin. If it had not been for the proleptical glimpse that God unveiled to me and my immediate family on that preceding Friday afternoon, I probably would be giving this account from a different institution, and with a different disposition. My wife and children can attest to the veracity of this account. This event happened on October 3, 1981, which was the first Saturday in October. It was a beautiful sunny day when I decided to take the family to lunch at a Chinese restaurant, which was located only five miles away from our home.

After enjoying the meal and preparing to leave the restaurant, we heard continuous loud claps of thunder and out of the large picture windows we saw very dark cloud formulations. It seemed that the storm rapidly appeared out of nowhere. We saw the torrential rains, and heard the wind whistling and tossing bushes, trash cans, and small trees throughout the parking lot. We thought that we were in the middle of a tornado or a dangerous microburst. My wife exclaimed, "Oh my goodness, we left several of our windows opened in the house, and my clothes outside on the back deck. Everything will be soaked or blown away!" When the storm subsided a little, we all quickly ran to the car, and started driving down the highway, trying to make it home before the storm intensified. Unfortunately, the storm intensified before leaving the parking lot. The wind was howling like a hurricane and the rain fell sideways. The car windshield wipers could not clear the windows fast enough. To make things worse, the drama escalated when one of my daughters began screaming. A small bush blew in front of the car and I had to swerve. She thought we were going to get into a serious accident and be killed. Nonetheless, I thought it best to continue driving through the storm. We were only a few miles away from home. As soon as we came to the entrance of our street, thankfully, the rain ceased. The wind stopped blowing, and the sun came back in its full array. When we finally reached our home, we quickly got out of the car and checked out our home and personal belongings.

We were amazed. We discovered that although rain water was rapidly flowing down both sides of our street, yet our house was completely dry. Remarkably, the clothes on the back deck were completely dry and not blown away. To our family's astonishment, our property—unlike our next door neighbor's—was also bone dry. My daughter Evette exclaimed, "Dad, look up there! There's a beautiful rainbow in the sky!" As we all looked in awe, we saw a double rainbow in all of its glory. We stared at the cloudless blue sky as the full spectrum of radiant colors was beaming in a perfect double rainbow. It was so vivid that it seemed as though God had spread a special covering over our home. All we could do was stand still and give glory to God.

I wondered what each of those unusual, but awe-inspiring manifestations in nature meant. I wondered what God was attempting to get me to understand or to see. The following Saturday, October 3, 1981, I found the answers. The meaning of those occurrences became crystal clear. I sensed that the phenomena were about to thrust me into another climactic experience with the strange darkness.

CHAPTER 21

The Corridor of Betrayal

ON THE AFTERNOON OF October 3rd a church meeting was convened by the moderator, in an attempt to bring a final resolution to the charges of misappropriation of building funds and other erroneous accusations. A few active members and a large group of people, whom I had never seen before, were also present. These people were invited by the disgruntled church members. Thankfully, the meeting was held in the church basement and not in the sanctuary. Someone informed me that the other folk were former church members, who had not been to the church since the beginning of my pastorate. If I were the moderator, they would have been required to leave the meeting because of their inactive status. However, they were permitted to remain as long as they remained silent. Needless to say, they refused to adhere, but vociferously began to espouse their own nefarious agenda. The church meeting escalated into a disgraceful, forty-five minute battle, initiated by the staff associate and his elderly cohorts.

Prior to the meeting, the Holy Spirit instructed me to watch, pray, and listen. I should only speak when he determined the time was appropriate. I watched, and silently prayed and listened for about forty-five minutes. In my mind's eye, I saw the church encircled by opposing gang members fighting for control of the church's turf. I saw old gang members pull out their guns, switch blades, and other weapons of warfare. I heard the viciousness in their voices as they argued face to face with one another. In my mind's eye, I saw old gang members punching and kicking each other in the face and in their lower extremities. Blood was flowing everywhere. I then felt the bitterness of hatred as a few individuals intensified the battle by standing up in my face, questioning my integrity, and casting aspersions about my character. People who really did not know me were shouting all manner of obscenities out of the darkness of those moments.

The strange darkness filled the entire room, and was drawing me into its destructive grip. My foot almost slipped! Neville the devil was fully primed to lash out and to verbally kill everyone in sight.

Immediately, a calmness enshrouded me like I had never before experienced. In that moment, the Holy Spirit opened my eyes and allowed me to see the depth of that darkness. The Holy Spirit gently spoke to my spirit, "Now is the time!" Peace descended upon my mind and heart; and in the midst of the tumultuous conflict and chaos the Holy Spirit empowered me to quietly walk up in front of the people. I calmed them all down, and then emphatically declared these words: "You will no longer be engaged in this disgraceful conflict. God will forgive you for everything you said and did in His house today. Nonetheless, with no malice in my heart, the Holy Spirit has led me to inform you that effective today, I am no longer assigned to remain as the pastor of this congregation."

I walked back to my wife, took her by the hand, and with our heads held high we walked out of the church. The Holy Spirit said to my spirit, "Do not look back, leave everything behind, and do not go back! The glory of the Lord has departed from this place." That Saturday afternoon, I walked out of that strange dark corridor into the light of a new corridor of hope and glory.

CHAPTER 22

The Corridor of Hope and Glory

HAVING GONE THROUGH SO many difficult storms signified to me that God was going to perform a supernatural, paradigmatic shift in my life and ministry. The double rainbow in the sky was a confirmation of the Lord's promise that He would always be present to walk with me through the storms and vicissitudes of life. Also, everything that was lost amidst the strange darkness would be restored. Everything the devil meant for evil Christ would reverse, and transform them into blessings to the glory of God. The path to this new corridor was unfolding before my eyes.

Saturday evening, I decided that I would leave the city of Brockton and return to Boston. I was determined either to accept an adjunct teaching position or to complete doctoral studies at one of the local theological schools. On Sunday morning, I arrived very early at the church. The sole intent was to read my formal resignation before the Messiah Baptist congregation. However, the moment I inserted the key into the front door of the First Parish Church building the Holy Spirit stopped me from entering, and spoke to my spirit.

It was clear as day, though provocative and unsettling. I heard the Holy Spirit say:

1. Rename the church building Mount Moriah.

2. Continue to stand as the pastor.

3. Preach and teach the gospel of Jesus Christ.

4. Trust God completely.

5. God will always be your (Jehovah Jireh) provider.

The moment had arrived as I stood behind the sacred desk. With my heart comingled with sorrow and joy, I humbly announced my resignation to the Messiah congregation. After a brief sigh, in obedience to the commission of the Holy Spirit, with trembling knees, I also announced the birth of Mount Moriah Baptist Church.

Shouts of praises to God, warm embraces, and sounds of relief reverberated throughout the sanctuary. We all experienced the *unspeakable joy of the Lord*. My mind immediately traveled back to the ominous manifestation of the double rainbow. It was as though Heaven came down and glory filled my soul. God always moves in mysterious and majestic ways. God's methods are always incomprehensible and unmatchable. Later that evening when everything had settled I was informed, to my amazement, that our new congregation was birthed on Sunday, October 4th—the same day as my birthday. I also learned that our church ground was the original training ground for revolutionary soldiers, and the place of origin for the city of Brocton. A double blessing. What a birthday gift. This decision brought peace to my soul.

CHAPTER 23

The Corridor of Peace

AFTER OUR SECOND YEAR of occupancy, we were blessed to purchase the church through the faithful contributions of our new congregation. We also received additional support from our sister church, Trinitarian Congregational in Wayland, Massachusetts, and The American Baptist Churches of Massachusetts (TABCOM). The Lord blessed us with a congregation of loving and faithful members. God also afforded us the privilege to oversee a multiplicity of holistic ministries within the city of Brockton and its greater communities. Throughout the years, Mount Moriah definitely had its challenges and anxious moments. The strange darkness raised its head every now and then, attempting to unsettle the business of the church. Although our resolve to stand firmly upon the principles of God's word was being attacked, yet the Holy Spirit always enabled us to stand unshakable and unmovable for thirty two years. As a congregation, we also gained confidence when we received the word of the Lord when he said:

> Peace I leave with you; my peace I give you. I do not give to you as the world gives. Do not let your hearts be troubled and do not be afraid. (John 14:27)

CHAPTER 24

The Corridor of Transformation

SERVING IN THE CAPACITY of senior pastor of Mount Moriah Baptist Church has given me the opportunity of gaining more insight into the core tenants of my faith. Through the years of study, and having wrestled with my own internal demons, I learned that there are very deep, dark places in the mind. There are regions where doubts, fear, and evil are birthed. Even though this is often dismissed by some as a nonsensical myth, nonetheless, there does exist a darker realm of reality unseen by natural vision, orchestrated by adversarial forces. Its unseen presence impacts the life of every human being on earth. The Holy Scripture reminds us:

> *Our struggle is not against flesh and blood, but against rulers, against the authorities, against the powers of this dark world and against the spiritual forces of evil in the heavenly realms.* (Eph 6:12)

As was mentioned earlier, there is nobody like God. Even though the darkness has an uncanny way of making unwanted, intrusive excursions into our thoughts, it always attempts to resurrect fear factors. This darkness accuses us of past failures, which often cause us to worry about inconsequential distractions and to make decisions based upon wrong assumptions.

Those wrong decisions can only lead to helplessness, hopelessness, and death. That is not the path God intended for any one of us. God's plan, designed thousands of years ago specifically for those who trust in Him, remains applicable for all believers today. The Holy Scripture declares:

> *"For I know the plans I have for you," declares the Lord,*
> *"plans to prosper you and not to harm you, plans to give*
> *you hope and a future." (Jer 29:11)*

The scripture also declares that even though we are sinners, yet Christ died for us. Why?—because of His amazing love for us.

Chapter 25

The Corridor of Love

WHEN ONE COMES TO a clearer understanding of just how much God loves us, and how uniquely we have been created, "grace" becomes amazing. By design, God crowned all humankind not only with the ability to achieve excellence, but he also endowed us with the unique capacity to concurrently span two dimensions of reality: the natural and the spiritual. Invariably, every human being on earth is destined to walk through each dimension. As we continue on our journey the quality of our life, as well as the eternal destination of our spirit and soul, are be determined by the personal choices we make. God did not leave us to traverse through these precarious dimensions as blind orphans or clueless, mindless animals.

The Holy Scriptures are replete with divinely inspired information. These scriptures explicitly unveil the guiding principles and precepts that are needed to teach us how we ought to live a balanced and prosperous life in today's world. If we are willing to embrace these truths, our safe pilgrimage through the temptations, the life-altering challenges, and the strange darkness will be assured. God will never fail us. He is working everything out for our good and for his glory, even though we cannot see the final outcome nor find answers to the question "Why me?" in the midst of the darkness of this world. God uses various means to get our full attention. This is necessary to keep us focused, and to continue walking on the right path that will ultimately lead to our divinely appointed destiny.

Our lives are encumbered by so many difficult situations that it becomes hard for some to believe that God really cares and loves them. Nonetheless, no matter how one may feel, God does love us. God's love for us is awesome, inexplicable, unconditional, and incomprehensible. The Holy Scripture unveils this truth about God, who said:

> *My thoughts are not your thoughts, neither are your ways my ways, saith the Lord. For as the heavens are higher than the earth, so are my ways higher than your ways and my thoughts than your thoughts.* (Isa 55:9)

Sometimes God uses the darkness to bless us immeasurably. Only God can change gross darkness into a glorious cosmic wonder. The greatest reversal in all of creation was not when God spoke to the darkness at creation when he said, "Let there be light." Rather, it was on that Friday afternoon on a hill called Calvary where God's one and only Son, Jesus the Christ, vicariously suffered, bled, and died for all of our sins.

That Friday was the strangest and darkest day on earth. However, early on the following Sunday morning, the strange darkness of death, hell, and the grave could not restrain the powerful and effulgent light of God. Jesus the Christ rose from the dead and broke every chain of the adversary. He arose from the grave with all power and authority in His hands, thereby assuring everyone who places authentic faith in Him that they also will have the ultimate victory over all powers and principalities in life. He also assured us that no weapons formed against us shall ever prevail. Through His ordeal He assured us of a number of things:

1. Nothing in all of creation shall ever again be able to separate us from His love.

2. No matter how difficult the circumstance or how hard the trial, we will win.

3. Death for the believer is not the end of life but rather is the grand entrance into new life.

This new life we now live will be in the presence of the glory of God. The light of God will eternally shine, always piercing through every dimension of darkness.

I have now come to another paradigmatic shift in my life. Like so many that have preceded me, I too share their same testimony. I once was young, but now I am old. I too have never seen the Lord forsake anyone who trusted in Him. With this understanding, I continue my pilgrimage with faith and hope, through the sequential corridors of life. I trust that you have not grown weary but will continue to walk with me one more step.

CHAPTER 26

The Corridor of Theft

MY JOURNEY THROUGH THE numerous corridors of life has taken me and my family to this pivotal juncture. I would like to share with you how these sequential corridors taught me how to cope optimistically with the new ophthalmic challenges in my life. My life-altering experiences came about in the form of an eye disease known as glaucoma (*the silent thief of sight*).

When I reached the age of forty, I went to a local community optometrist and received a general eye examination in order to obtain a pair of reading glasses. After a few cursory tests, the doctor informed me that I had borderline glaucoma. I considered it to be just another phase in the natural process of aging. At that time the only prescribed recommendation was a stronger pair of reading glasses.

As the years rapidly passed, I noticed that my vision was diminishing. Rather than seek medical attention, I concluded that this was no big deal but just another one of those physical occurrences common to everyone over forty. I surmised that the only needed action to take was to acquire stronger reading glasses. I had deemed other things to be of a higher priority. For that reason, I never purchased the glasses, nor did I take the time to have my eyes reexamined until many years later. Throughout the many years of pastoral ministry, my conclusions remained the same. As far as I could tell, there were no apparent ophthalmological changes beyond my normal diminished vision. However, it was not until I rearranged my priorities, set aside my prognostications, and consented to be examined by an ophthalmologist that I discovered that my self-diagnoses were incorrect. I was informed that the pressure levels of both eyes were extremely high and if left untreated could inevitably lead to permanent blindness.

I was diagnosed with an extremely severe condition called *primary angle closure glaucoma*. It was explained to me that this ocular disease was serious. The ophthalmologist, in her attempt to be certain that I understood the serious nature of my condition, restated it in terms that were easier for me to comprehend. In layman terms she said:

> *The eyes naturally produce fluids behind the eyes that flow through very fine veins into a drainage channel. This channel allows the fluids to flow effortlessly out of the eyes. Glaucoma partially clogs these channels hindering the normal drainage, thereby increasing the buildup of eye fluid and pressure resulting in irreparable damage to the optic nerve. Comparatively, it was like attaching a garden hose to a turned on fire hydrant: inevitably the garden hose would be severely impaired, beyond repair, destroyed.*

My condition required immediate medical intervention. I clearly understood her analogy and accepted her recommendation to begin treatment. She assured me that although glaucoma remained incurable, nonetheless, there were new technologies and eye drops that were effective in arresting its advancement. This new ordeal was another faith stretching experience in my corridors of strange darkness.

Chapter 27

The Corridor of Blindness

The thought of becoming permanently blind is traumatic and could easily have thrust me into a state of depression and despair. If it had not been for those earlier sequential corridors, I probably would not have had the fortitude to walk with confidence through this new corridor. This silent thief, called glaucoma, after it does its damage, engenders all kinds of feelings because it can also dramatically alter every day existence. Many of the normal everyday freedoms and activities I had taken for granted had either been curtailed or diminished. Within a four year period I underwent a multiplicity of eye examinations, intrusive eye surgeries, and numerous intravitreal injections. I had so many pictures taken of my eyeballs that I felt as though I had a large portfolio sufficient to submit to an eye beauty contest. There were times when I had to stare into a light that was brighter than the noon-day sun.

There was another examination called the *visual field test*. This test was not only painless but frustrating. It is used to detect the extent of damage impacting the central or peripheral vision. For about ten minutes, I had to stare into a computerized machine keeping my eye focused on a tiny dark spot located in the center of a white screen. For a moment, I felt as though I was ushered into the center of deep space. I was further instructed to press a hand-held clicker each time I saw a tiny flashing white pin of light. There were times when I was able to see every tiny dot and other times when I saw nothing. There were also times when I was going stare crazy and began clicking at everything I thought was moving. This test was essential for the doctors because it helped them measure, monitor, and control the extent of damage occurring in my eyes. I was glad when that test was over. However, there would be numerous other tests.

In an attempt to lower the extremely high pressure in my eyes, a myriad of eye drops were prescribed and applied. For years, my eyes were anointed with prescribed medications. Only doctors and pharmacologists could pronounce the names of these medications. Fortunately, each of the bottled medication tops was color coded. Sometimes the drops were effective and other times they were not. The medication and dosage had to be increased. I graduated from having to take two medications three times per day to over six medications. There were times when I had to take multiple drops every hour of the day for many weeks. I had to devise an anointing book just to keep track of the proper times and anointing dosages. I am so glad I did. A time had come when the eye drops were no longer sufficient, and laser surgery became the most viable option.

CHAPTER 28

The Corridor of Humor and Treatment

I FOUND IT AMUSING that God would use unique and sometimes humorous means to help me rise above my challenging situations. As I thought about some of my experiences, there were several comical occurrences that reminded me of Mr. Magoo. Mr. Magoo was a television cartoon character that I watched as a child.

The famous adventures of Mr. Magoo featured an incredibly wealthy, cantankerous, baldheaded old man who had a severe ophthalmic condition of nearsightedness. He was constantly driving his old car or walking blindly into precarious situations. His vision was so severely diminished that he never saw danger or anything clear in his view. Everyone and everything else was always out of order. Nothing was more important to him than fulfilling his own agenda or completing his mission. It was a miracle that he was never hurt or intentionally tried to hurt someone else. No matter the situation, he always came through it laughing. He was a hilarious cartoon character. Strange things can happen when one's vision is diminished.

On one occasion my nephew Kevin was driving me to a scheduled appointment with my ophthalmologist, when I encountered a unique scene. I looked out of the side window and I thought I saw three remarkably large Clydesdale horses grazing in the countryside pasture. Astonished, I said to Kevin, "Did you see that?" He said, "See what?" I said, "Over there! Take the next turn—we have to check that out. Those were the largest Clydesdale horses I had ever seen." He chuckled and said, "Over there? Those aren't horses, those are brown houses." Over the course of the next five miles we laughed and joked about other things that appeared to emerge out of this strange new darkness. This venture also caused me to realize how severely impaired the peripheral vision in my right eye had become. Like Mr. Magoo, things that were seen were not what they appeared to be.

Another comical moment happened while driving in my golf cart with my wife, Ruth. We were jetting down a designated path in the Legends Country Club. Suddenly I stopped the cart and with great concern asked Ruth, "What's happening in front of us? Who are those people waving to us?" With a strange look on her face she turned to me and said, "What people?" I replied, "Those people over there, standing in the pathway." When we drove about ten yards Ruth said, "Gene, you're crazy. Move over, and let me drive." What I thought were people waving to us were not people at all. It was just the bushes along the side of the pathway, swaying back and forth in a gentle breeze. We both started laughing. However, in the midst of our laughter I said to myself, it must also be time for me to turn in my car keys and stop driving. It might be time for me to consider moving to the next level of healing. These short adventures caused me to see beyond the humorous similarity I shared with Mr. Magoo. Instead, it caused me to consider a somewhat parallel experience with a man who had an ophthalmic condition recorded in the New Testament gospels.

The biblical record asserts that a blind man was brought to the Lord. Jesus touched his eyes, and his sight was partially restored. Jesus asked the man, "What do you see?" He responded, "I see men walking as trees." Jesus then touched him again, and the man's distorted vision was completely restored. The man began to see everything with perfect clarity. By this time it had become apparent to me that I had some serious visual impairments. If I was ever going to retain my vision, I knew that I too needed another healing touch by God's appointed ophthalmic surgeon.

These next sequential corridors were sometimes frustrating, stressful, irritating, bewildering, humorous, humbling, and inspiring. For several years, I went through various intrusive eye surgeries. I had numerous intravitreal eyeball injections. I shudder to recall my first eyeball injection experience. Honestly, I thought that I had been wrongly escorted into the laboratory of Doctor Frankenstein.

Prior to the surgical experience, I was not apprehensive, because the anesthesiologist was reassuring about the surgery. Although I would be awake throughout the operation I nonetheless would experience no pain. That was good news to me. However, neither he nor the attending associates prepared me for what was to follow. I did not find out until after I was on the operating table. My entire face was covered with a special surgical mask, exposing only my eye. Lights that appeared to be as bright as the morning sun were pulled down above my head. Then out of the corner of my eye I saw the surgeon approach me with an injection needle. I thought he was going to use it to inject novocain into my jaw to further numb my eye. Instead, I was shocked almost out of my socks. He inserted and twisted the needle straight into my eyeball! I was terrified. I remember clutching the table in total disbelief.

To my further astonishment, I saw him approach me again with another needle. Before he stuck me again I yelled out, "Not again?" He responded, "Do you feel any pain?" With trembling in my voice I said, "No, but I really don't want to see or feel anything!" He instructed the anesthesiologist to apply additional medicine, and then proceeded to inject my eyeball two more times. I was traumatized by that experience and vowed to myself that it would never happen like that again. However, since that day I had to experience many more injections but rest assured that in every situation, before the doctor was permitted to proceed, they were expected to first answer my questions. Since that notable day, I have undergone about twenty seven intravitreal eyeball injections

Moreover, I had laser surgeries (*light amplification by stimulated emission of radiation*), cataracts removed from both eyes; and a trabeculectomy inserted in my right eye *("a piece of tissue in the drainage section of the eye is removed, creating a new opening which allows fluid to drain out of the eye, bypassing the clogged drainage channels of the tiny mesh channels thus releasing the fluid to drain into the blood stream.")* Due to the severity of the glaucoma in my right eye, and the ineffectiveness of numerous medications to lower the eye pressure, it was deemed timely to have what is called a Baerveldt implant. This procedure involved placing a flexible silicone drainage pouch in the eye. This device was designed to enhance drainage through the eye's natural system, sustaining the subsequent reduction of the eye pressure. The operation was very successful, and dramatically reduced the eye pressure.

While I was in Boston, Massachusetts, the retina specialist discovered another reason why, despite the aggressive treatments, my vision was diminishing rather than improving. This was now attributable to the development of what is called a "macular hole." It was explained to me that a "macular hole develops when the nerve cells of the macular becomes separated from each other, and pull away from the back surface of the eye." To correct this condition would require additional eye surgery. The nature of this surgery also required strict adherence to post-operative healing measures. Non-adherence could result in serious outcomes. It sounded to me as though I had to prepare myself for another major battle getting ready to take place within my eyes and mind. When the doctor further explained the nature of the surgery and meticulous recovery process, I adamantly refused to accept that option. From my perspective, I would have to place myself in an untenable and incapacitating position for a prolonged period of time. I could not believe what I was hearing.

It was at this juncture that I invited my wife to come into the doctor's office to verify whether I had heard him correctly. The doctor restated the entire procedure. My wife confirmed the doctor's explanation; we looked at each other and she agreed with my decision. She said, "That sounds ridiculous. It is unlikely that his active schedule and lifestyle could accommodate those requirements." If the truth be told, I had no intention of trying to adjust my schedule to synchronize with that type of surgery. No matter what the doctor said or anyone else thought, to me that constituted cruel and unusual punishment.

The surgical aspect was not the problem. The difficulty lay with the post-operative requirements and potential side effects. When I heard the doctor restate information to my wife, it was as though every past voice, every past image and imagination from the past, jumped as a gang style into my mind. I sensed that this was going to be another defining moment that I had to fight.

Even though the doctor spoke softly and apologetically, foolishly, I immediately jumped to my feet and said, "You must think I'm crazy? There is no way that I could think of submitting to that kind of procedure." Sarcastically I said, "No way, no shape, no how!" Truthfully, in my mind the darkness of pride had risen. It caused me to prematurely conclude that my ability to fulfill many other pressing responsibilities would be delimited or become nullified. I also thought that it would radically alter my present state of wellbeing. Therefore, I felt justified in my decision not to undergo this type of surgery.

Perhaps you will agree with or at least understand the reason for my decision. The following outlines what the post-operative healing procedure would entail. Surgically, a gas bubble would be inserted inside the eye. The purpose of the insertion was to maintain a proper amount of pressure to float against the macular, gradually sealing the hole. After several months, the gas bubble would slowly dissipate and the macular hole would be resealed. However, in order for the post-surgery to be successful, it would be imperative I strictly adhere to the post-operative healing measures. These measures required that I lay prostrate, remaining as still as possible, with the head in a face down position for approximately twenty hours each day, for a period of several weeks. In some cases it might take weeks or a few months for the gas bubble to completely dissipate. Vision misalignment and color distortions could also become other temporary post-operative side effects. Having previewed the various support equipment provided little consolation. I was not certain whether it was fear or pride that helped me to decide that this procedure was a nonviable option.

Two years later, while in Florida, I noticed a significant change in my central vision, so I sought the opinions of other retina specialists. After multiple examinations, it appeared as though the retina membranes had experienced something that looked similar to a serious volcanic eruption. The normal membranes should look like a smooth plain, but mine looked instead like hills, valleys, and mountains. The doctors informed me that blindness was imminent unless I underwent an eye operation known as vitreo retinal surgery. For me, it was that same dreaded "gas bubble" operation. I began to sense that uncanny intrusion of fear and pride. However, in 2012, I successfully underwent both the vitreo-retinal surgery and epiretirial membrane surgery. Although the glaucoma was aggressively monitored and treated, the prognosis still remained poor.

The question one might ask is, "How did you make it through that trying vitreo-retinal ordeal?" It was not easy. Truthfully, it was only by the grace of God and a supportive wife. The Lord had to radically adjust my thinking and attitude. Pride, anger, and fear were removed; in its place my thoughts were brought under control and shifted to a place of remembrance. Each hour as I lay prostrate across a small bench in my living room. I began to remember the painful experiences but joyful testimonies of my sisters, brother, and close friends who persevered through their struggles, although they lay dying from an incurable cancer. They kept their faith, because it was deeply rooted in the reality of God's will and presence. They held onto what was written in the scriptures, "God is a present help in the time of trouble." Therefore, they never yielded to their fears, nor surrendered their hope.

I was deeply humbled, and at the same time immeasurably inspired by those precious remembrances. I realized how foolish and prideful I had been. In comparison to their health challenges, my tests were only gentle setbacks. Those remembrances helped me to face my fear, swallow my pride, and endure my cross. Throughout those strange hours, days, and weeks, as I continued to remain immobile and confined to the living room or bed room, the negative thoughts that desperately tried to arise were repressed by unending gospel songs and hymns that arose in my spirit. I also sensed the inspiring prayers of my family and friends encouraging me to "hold onto God's unchanging hand." Momentarily, the strange darkness might have knocked me down but it did not knock me out.

After going through the surgeries, daily eye anointing, and months of follow-up examinations, the advancement of glaucoma has been minimalized, and the retina in both eyes is healing. Overall the surgeries were very successful. Although my vision remains diminutive and I see everything differently, I nevertheless can still see.

One interesting new thing I have discovered about my diminished sight is that on a daily basis I observe things like Mr. Magoo. A variety of unusual, comical, optical illusions continue to appear before me. I think others might interpret these episodes as the strange products of my imagination, but to me they were and still remain laughable moments. The glaucoma specialist explained to me that this could be a temporary post-operation side effect. He further explained that during the healing process of the macular, the optic nerve (which impacts the central vision) is attempting to reestablish connectivity with the brain. While transitioning, the process will sometimes produce image discolorations and visual misalignments. My affinity with Mr. Magoo was now clarified. I found similar visual irregularities happening to me. Interestingly, fluorescent and incandescent lights, as well as natural daylight, each produce its own optical illusion. Moreover, every time I enter a large store lit by brilliant fluorescent light my eyes immediately transition. It is as though the pupils of my eyes open wider, thereby permitting an overabundance of radiant light to burst in.

The optical effect that is produced as I looked at people of different ethnicities and clothing hues was both strange and humorous. At first glance, everyone appeared to be either faceless or headless. People who were white or fair skinned, especially if they happened not to be wearing bright or colorful clothing, sometimes appeared to look ghostly, like Casper the friendly ghost. Conversely, although I was able to hear the voices of people of dark complexion, they became shadowy figures in the brightness of the light, particularly if they happened to wear dark or black clothing.

Throughout the year, I have had many unsettling moments. Whenever my wife and I would go out to a restaurant for dinner, and the restaurant happened to be dimly lit, I would experience a strange optical illusion. This optical illusion would manifest whenever the servers were dressed in black attire. Sometimes I could only see the person's head coming to my table with the food tray floating in the air. Sometimes I closed my eyes and bowed my head, not out of fear but to prevent myself from laughing out loud in the person's presence. However, one disconcerting note about this unexpected ordeal was that I could not always discern what food I was about to eat. That was an optical illusion I no longer wish to experience.

Walking through this corridor with severely diminished vision was not always laced with laughable moments. There were times when I became frustrated and upset with the condition. When I am at home, the incandescent lighting raises a set of new daily challenges relative to the rapid disappearance of objects. The furniture in my home predominately is black. Strategically, I placed several large yellow flashlights in different sections of the house— but not because I was fearful of falling. It was due to the fact that every time I placed an object down, I found myself playing the childhood game of hide and go seek for about fifteen minutes. The flash lights curtailed the long search.

Considering everything I had already been through, these ventures were something entirely new. I would no longer just be contending with the precarious strange darkness. Now I would be learning how to cope with the various effects that light would have upon my vision. These new experiences became another step in the process of my spiritual, emotional, and physical healing.

CHAPTER 29

The Corridor of Healing

As my sufferings mounted I soon realized that there were two ways in which I could respond to my situation—either to react with bitterness or seek to transform the suffering into a creative force. I decided to follow the latter course.—Martin Luther King, Jr.[1]

I'm here. I love you. I don't care if you need to stay up crying all night long, I will stay with you. There's nothing you can ever do to lose my love. I will protect you until you die, and after your death I will still protect you. I am stronger than Depression and I am braver than Loneliness and nothing will ever exhaust me.—Elizabeth Gilbert[2]

ALL OF US AT some point in our lives will yearn for physical or spiritual healing. The prophet Isaiah announced that one of the salvific manifestations of the Messiah of God would be to usher in eternal peace and spiritual healing for the people of God. Speaking of Christ, he said:

---

1. Washington, *A Testament of* Hope, p. 41.
2. Gilbert, *Eat, Pray, Love,* p. 54.

The Corridor of Healing

He was pierced for our transgressions, he was crushed for our iniquities; the punishment that brought us peace was on him, and by his wounds we are healed. (Isa 53:5)

I am pleased to say that I am still in the process of healing. The rapid advancement of glaucoma has been slowed down. I still have a few residual ophthalmic challenges. I continue to anoint my eyes daily in order to effectively maintain normal eye pressures. Although the privilege to drive my car has been curtained, it has not stopped me from participating in a wide variety of creative activities and other meaningful ventures.

I wish I could say that the illusive shadows of darkness have totally dissipated, but that would be misleading and untrue. The adversary leaves us alone but only for a brief season—then it comes back with intense vengeance. However, my mind, heart, and soul have been made whole by the "healing wounds" of Jesus Christ. Although the struggles and vicissitudes in this life may continue, they nonetheless have been stripped of their capacity to paralyze me with fear. The purpose of my life has become clearer. At this particular season in my life, I am no longer trying to identify illusive shadows or run away from painful realities of life. Instead, there still remains deep inside of me a yearning that beckons me to live out the remaining years of my life, not in vain, but in a manner pleasing to God. Also, I still have a burning passion to be of help to somebody.

CHAPTER 30

The Corridor of the Unknown

AS ONE TRANSITIONS THROUGH one's "golden years," one discovers the interesting phenomenon of becoming more sensitive to the rapidity of life. The inevitable physical and unexpected emotional alterations of being old, and the real sense of the emerging, inescapable, enigmatic, strange corridor that is ahead—the unwelcomed intrusion of death—become increasingly central to life

Some believe this season to be the final corridor that provides for an immediate escape from the vicissitudes of life, and that is the end. Consequently, some elect to prematurely terminate their earthly existence. Others, who have not lost hope in God, continue their journey through this corridor, continuing to believe that this is a transitional channel leading into the ultimate corridor of glory.

Job, that ancient saint, set an example for all of us to emulate. He demonstrated the essence of what it means to persevere and what faith looks like when life thrusts one unexpectedly into the world of devastating ordeals and loss. In spite of the loss of everything, Job was still able to proclaim:

> *Though he slay me, yet will I hope in him . . . I know that*
> *my redeemer lives, and that in the end he will stand on*
> *the earth. And after my skin has been destroyed, yet in my*

flesh I will see God. I, myself will see him with my own
eyes—I, and not another. How my heart yearns within me!
(Job 13:15, 19:25–27)

Philosophically and theologically, I have come to believe that this corridor, through which I now walk, is an earthly temporal place. This place is one in which all of our life experiences coalesce in order to prepare us for the last corridor. Into this transitional corridor all of our questions, doubts, fears, disappointments, troubles, strange imaginations, dreams, aspirations, blessings, and beliefs mysteriously conjoin, ultimately validating what we believe. It is there where the Holy Spirit examines the authenticity of our faith, and strengthens us to continue trusting in the One in whom we place our confidence to save our souls. This corridor defines and gives meaning to the "real me." Stepping into this strange, seemingly dark, long, and lonely corridor is similar to the dimension invoked by the psalmist who tells us that "Deep calls to deep." (Ps 42:7)

The corridor into which I presently walk, even though it might not be my final corridor, is one that I refer to as the "Corridor of the Unknown."

Sometimes in our moments of perplexity, we tend to feel like another sacred writer: one who looked at all of the circumstances that enshrouded his life and then asked God to unveil to him how long he had to live. In the same breath he also asked, when and how he was to die. He prayed to God:

> *Show me, LORD, my life's end and the number of my*
> *days; let me know how fleeting my life is. You have made*
> *my days a mere handbreadth; the span of my years is as*
> *nothing before you.* (Ps 39:4–5)

Longevity of life and immunity to its troubles are promised to no one. God in His infinite wisdom veiled the eyes of the sacred inquirer, just as He still veils our eyes today. God foreknew that if that level of information was revealed, it would cause some people to become overwhelmed by fear and to prematurely give up on life. Instead, God graciously determined that the people of God must trust Him and live by faith. The people of God must live with the inner conviction that all of their days remain in His capable hands. They should live with the understanding and assurance that all of the perplexities and trials of life are being reshaped and redirected for their ultimate wellbeing. In other words, as another wise man from antiquity said:

> Trust in the Lord with all your heart and lean not on your
> own understanding
> In all your ways submit to him,
> and he will make your paths straight. (Prov 3:5–6)

As I continue my pilgrimage through the corridor of the unknowable, I pause on each step of the way to meditate on each of those essential truths. Although the silent thief (glaucoma) continues to slowly advance, yet there is no additional surgery in sight. The medicated treatments are at their maximum, and there is no guarantee that these treatments will always be effective. Nevertheless, I will continue to apply eye drops daily my eyes daily, and trust that they will maintain the low pressures.

Even though it now appears that during this season of my life I have to deal with the real possibility of becoming totally blind, I still remain hopeful that one day God will act and I will once again be able to see.

I am fully cognizant that in order for my wife and family members to adjust to my loss of sight that new proactive measures have to be undertaken. This requires:

1. Developing a daily strategic action plan

2. Identifying resources designed to assist persons with low vision

3. Making our home more user–friendly

4. Receiving professional counseling services

CHAPTER 31

The Corridor of Victory

IN CONCLUSION, PRAYER, WHEN uttered in humility and with authentic faith in Almighty God, has incomprehensible and immeasurable power. This eternal truism was unveiled to the world long ago by the Lord Jesus Christ. He stated that, *"Again I say to you, if two of you agree on earth about anything they ask, it will be done for them by my Father in heaven."* (Matt 18:19) The great apostolic benediction of Saint Paul also exemplifies this fact:

> *Now to him who is able to do immeasurably more than all we ask or imagine, according to his power that is at work within us, to him be glory in the church and in Christ Jesus throughout all generations, forever and ever! Amen.* (Eph 3:20–21)

Each person has been endowed with the capacity to make choices. However, some choices we make are wise, while others are not so wise. Nonetheless, the choices we make often determine the longevity or quality of our lives. Apart from an unexpected accident or a nefarious act of violence enacted upon us, we can choose to walk with and by faith, or become emotionally paralyzed by fear or anger. We can choose to die in a state of helplessness or to live victorious with hopeful expectations. The Holy Scripture clearly states in Prov 14:12: *There is a way which seemeth right to man, but the end thereof are the ways of death.* God's desire for all of humanity is that we are willing to choose life:

> Today I have given you the choice between life and death, between blessings and curses. Now I call on heaven and earth to witness the choice you make. Oh, that you would choose life, so that you and your descendants might live! (Deut 30:19)

In harmony with this scripture, William Arthur Dunkerley, a prolific 20th century poet, penned these thought-provoking words in his poem, "The Ways":

> To every man there openeth
> A Way, and Ways, and a Way,
> And the High Soul climbs the High Way,
> And the Low Soul gropes the Low,
> And, in between, on the misty flats,
> The rest drift to and fro.
> But to every man there openeth
> A High Way, and a Low.
> And every man decideth
> The Way his soul shall go.[1]

The choice remains ours. While we still have the breath of life silently pulsating through our lungs, and while we still have activity in our brain and can think with a clear mind, wisdom beckons us to choose life. The greater life can only be found in Jesus Christ who is the Way, the Truth, and the Life.

Thank you for patiently walking with me all of the way through my many sequential corridors. It is my earnest prayer that as you continue on your own journey, contending with your strange darkness, that you will never become discouraged to the point of losing hope. Always remember that God loves you. The Lord Jesus Christ will always be a present help in the midst of your darkest moments, and the Holy Spirit will enable you to persevere through any and all human reversals and infirmities. God will

---

1. Dunkerley, William Arthur, "The Ways."

be glorified, and your strange darkness will become as a fleeting shadow. Do not be afraid to walk by faith and not by sight. Soon, one day, we will all be able to share our testimony together:

We once were blind, but now, we see! Hallelujah!

About the Author

Rev. Eugene L. Neville is the retired pastor and founder of the Mount Moriah Baptist Church, Inc. in Brockton, Massachusetts. He served with distinction in the Christian ministry for over forty five years. He has developed and implemented numerous ministries utilizing technology not only for his congregation, but also assisting other churches across the country. Rev. Neville has taught and mentored over twenty men and women in preparation for ministry. He served as the first Project Director of the Black Church Capacity Building Program for a leading philanthropic foundation in Boston, Massachusetts. Rev. Neville is also one of the founding members of the Center for Urban Ministerial Education in Boston.

For several years Rev. Neville served on various boards within the greater Brockton community. He left the city of Brockton with a rich legacy by establishing the Amara Computer Learning Center, the Emergency Food Programs for the homeless, and a Home Goods Distribution Ministry for the needy. He also developed the Prison Family Reunification Ministry in order to help reintegrate former inmates into their homes, work force, and community. Lastly, he and his wife developed the Higher Education Research Center, which is a program designed to assist socially and economically marginalized youths prepare for and gain entrance into college. Rev. Neville is a man with a vision and a commitment to encourage and empower people to live above their human constrictions.

About the Author

In 1973, Rev. Eugene L. Neville graduated from Gordon-Conwell Theological Seminary where he earned the Master of Divinity degree. He and his wife Ruth are the proud parents of two daughters, Evette and Evonne, and have five grandchildren. Eugene and Ruth presently reside in the city of Clermont, Florida.

Bibliography

Braxton, Joanne M., ed. *The Collected Poetry of Paul Lawrence Dunbar.* Charlottesville: University of Virginia Press, 1993.

Dunkerley, William Arthur. "The Ways." http://www.public-domain-poetry. com/william-arthur-dunkerley.

Holland, Josiah Gilbert. *Garnered Sheaves: the Complete Poetical Works of J. G. Holland.* New York: Scribner, Armstrong & Co., 1873.

King, Martin Luther Jr., *Strength to Love.* New York: Walker & Company, 1963.

Lowell, James Russell. *Poems of James Russell Lowell.* New York: Thomas Y. Crowell Co., 1892.

McClatchy, J. D., ed. *Henry Wadsworth Longfellow: Poems and Other Writings.* New York: Library of America, 2000.

Washington, James M. *A Testament of Hope: the Essential Writings of Speeches of Martin Luther King, Jr.* New York: HarperCollins, 1986.